Black
Achievement
IN SCIENCE

Physics

MC

Mason Crest

Black
Achievement
IN SCIENCE

Biology

Chemistry

Computer Science

Engineering

Environmental Science

Inventors

Medicine

Physics

Space

Technology

Black
Achievement
IN SCIENCE

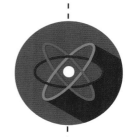

Physics

By DIANE BAILEY
Foreword by Malinda Gilmore and Mel Poulson,
National Organization for the Advancement of
Black Chemists and Chemical Engineers

Mason Crest
450 Parkway Drive, Suite D
Broomall, PA 19008
www.masoncrest.com

Series ISBN: 978-1-4222-3554-6
Hardback ISBN: 978-1-4222-3562-1
EBook ISBN: 978-1-4222-8329-5

First printing
1 3 5 7 9 8 6 4 2

Produced by Shoreline Publishing Group LLC
Santa Barbara, California
Editorial Director: James Buckley Jr.
Designer: Patty Kelley
Production: Sandy Gordon
www.shorelinepublishing.com
Cover photographs by Monkey Business Images/Dreamstime.com.

Library of Congress Cataloging-in-Publication Data

Names: Bailey, Diane, 1966- author.
Title: Physics / by Diane Bailey ; foreword by Malinda Gilmore, Ph. D., Executive Board Chair, and Mel
    Poulson, Executive Board Vice-Chair, National Organization for the Professional Advancement of Black
    Chemists and Chemical Engineers (NOBCChE).
Description: Broomall, PA : Mason Crest, an imprint of National Highlights, Inc., [2017] | "2017 | Series:
    Black achievement in science | Includes bibliographical references and index.
Identifiers: LCCN 2016002447| ISBN 9781422235621 (hardback) | ISBN 1422235629 (hardback) | ISBN
    9781422235546 (series) | ISBN 1422235548 (series) | ISBN 9781422283295 (ebook) | ISBN 1422283291
    (ebook)
Subjects: LCSH: African American physicists--Biography--Juvenile literature. | African American scien-
    tists--Biography--Juvenile literature. Classification: LCC QC15 .B34 2017 | DDC 530.092/396073--dc23
LC record available at http://lccn.loc.gov/2016002447

Contents

Key Icons to Look for

Words to Understand: These words with their easy-to-understand definitions will increase the reader's understanding of the text, while building vocabulary skills.

Research Projects: Readers are pointed toward areas of further inquiry connected to each chapter. Suggestions are provided for projects that encourage deeper research and analysis.

Text-Dependent Questions: These questions send the reader back to the text for more careful attention to the evidence presented here.

Series Glossary of Key Terms: This back-of-the-book glossary contains terminology used throughout this series. Words found here increase the reader's ability to read and comprehend higher-level books and articles in this field.

Educational Videos: Readers can view videos by scanning our QR codes, providing them with additional educational content to supplement the text. Examples include news coverage, moments in history, speeches, iconic moments, and much more!

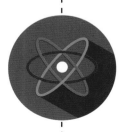

cience, Technology, Engineering and Mathematics (STEM) are vital to our future, the future of our country, the future of our regions, and the future of our children. STEM is everywhere and it shapes our everyday experiences. Science and technology have become the leading foundation of global development. Both subjects continue to improve the quality of life as new findings, inventions, and creations emerge from the basis of science. A career in a STEM discipline is a fantastic choice and one that should be explored by many.

In today's society, STEM is becoming more diverse and even internationalized. However, the shortage of African Americans and other minorities, including women, still exists. This series—***Black Achievement in Science***—reveals the numerous career choices and pathways that great African-American scientists, technologists, engineers, and mathematicians

By Malinda Gilmore, NOBCChE Executive Board Chair and Mel Poulson, NOBCChE Executive Board Vice-Chair

have pursued to become successful in a STEM discipline. The purpose of this series of books is to inspire, motivate, encourage, and educate people about the numerous career choices and pathways in STEM. We applaud the authors for sharing the experiences of our forefathers and foremothers and ultimately increasing the number of people of color in STEM and, more specifically, increasing the number of African Americans to pursue careers in STEM.

The personal experiences and accomplishments shared within are truly inspiring and gratifying. It is our hope that by reading about the lives and careers of these great scientists, technologists, engineers, and mathematicians, the reader might become inspired and totally committed to pursue a career in a STEM discipline and say to themselves, "If they were able to do it, then I am definitely able to do it, and this, too, can be me." Hopefully, the reader will realize that these great accomplishments didn't come easily. It was because of hard work, perseverance, and determination that these chosen individuals were so successful.

As Executive Board Members of The National Organization for the Professional Advancement of Black Chemists and Chemical Engineers (NOBCChE) we are excited about this series. For more than 40 years, NOBCChE has promoted the STEM fields and its mission is to build an eminent cadre of people of color in STEM. Our mission is in line with the overall purpose of this series and we are indeed committed to inspiring our youth to explore and contribute to our country's future in science, technology, engineering, and mathematics.

We encourage all readers to enjoy the series in its entirety and identify with a personal story that resonates well with you. Learn more about that person and their career pathway, and you can be just like them. with you. Learn more about that person and their career pathway, and you can be just like them.

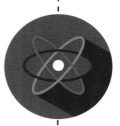

he universe is a very no-nonsense ruler. Actually, it is a bit of a dictator. It operates by a specific set of rules, which we call the laws of physics. It enforces these laws very strictly. They cannot be broken—it is impossible. They are also very far reaching. They apply to everyone and everything and everywhere.

Enormous black holes are spinning in the outer reaches of the universe, billions of light years away. Tiny quarks—less than 0.00000000000000001 meters long—are vibrating inside the protons and neutrons of atoms. All of them, regardless of size or power, follow the laws of physics.

The electrons and protons that swirl invisibly form and build all matter.

Physics explains why hot things always cool off.

It explains why the speed of light is always the same.

It explains why what goes up always comes down—on Earth, at least.

It may be comforting to see the word "always" so much, or it may be intimidating. Either way, it is not going anywhere. In physics, there are no exceptions. This does not mean there are no contradictions or mysteries in physics. In fact, there are plenty. Physicists struggle to understand why one set of equations can describe the actions of some things, but does not work on others. The problem here is not physics, though—it's the limits of human understanding.

Physics is often called the most basic of all the sciences. Chemistry and biology also explain how natural systems work and interact, but they are still based on the fundamental laws of physics. Without these underpinnings, none of it makes sense.

Over thousands of years, humans have learned to adapt to the laws of physics without even thinking about it. We know that it hurts when falling objects hit us on the head, but we rarely put it in the form of an equation about acceleration. We know that machines get hot when they operate, but we don't usually explain it in terms of thermodynamics.

Over those same thousands of years, though, there have been people who thought deeply about such things—and more. They asked questions such as: How did the universe begin? Where and when do space and time merge together? Why does matter sometimes act like it's a bunch of particles, while other times it moves in waves? Why does matter even matter? Does a star exploding trillions of miles away have any significance in our lives?

As scientists have probed into the laws of physics, they have learned more details about how they work. Those discoveries have made enormous impacts on our lives. Knowledge of physics is critical to understanding how machines operate, for example. Without it, humans would not have been able to invent an airplane that would actually stay in

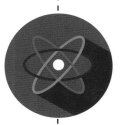

the air. The flight of an airplane may seem to defy the laws of gravity. In truth, it uses a complex blend of other physical laws to simply overcome it—at least for a little while.

Ever wonder how architects can build skyscrapers that are more than a hundred stories tall? It's because they understand how physics can be used to manage such enormous weight and stress. How about those high-performance sneakers? Their design is based on how different materials act under different conditions. Physics is always there, governing things that usually get very little attention. Take ketchup, for example. If you've ever tried to get stubborn ketchup out of a bottle, you know that shaking the bottle helps. That's because stress (shaking) makes the fluid runnier, so that it flows more easily—and that's all physics. The list goes on, from X-rays and electricity to cars and cell phones. Virtually every invention and advancement in technology can be traced back to people who had a thorough understanding of physics.

Many of the most recognized names in physics—Isaac Newton, Albert Einstein, Stephen Hawking—are those of white men. Historically, careers in the sciences have been mostly limited to white people, especially men. Even within the sciences, physics is among the most difficult fields to get into, and that's especially true for African Americans. Unfortunately, they have endured decades of discrimination, particularly in the United States. This has nothing to do with intelligence or ability; instead, it's about opportunity and attitude. Studying physics requires a lot of educa-

tion in science and math, and many people of color simply have not had those opportunities and when they did, they often faced prejudice from others who did not believe they could do the job.

The work of physics professionals often touches different aspects of science.

In spite of these hardships, there are exceptional black people who have achieved great things in science, both in America and abroad. Although most scientists do not become famous, that does not make their contributions less important. Each scientist's work adds another piece to the puzzle. Each viewpoint and research discovery helps shape our overall understanding. Black physicists have made vital contributions to this body of knowledge. The ones profiled in this book are examples of people who have worked over, through, or around racial barriers. Some were pioneers in the field, proving that the pursuit of knowledge is open to everyone, regardless of race. Others have built on the discoveries made by earlier scientists. In any case, they all show that advances in science are a team effort. The laws of society sometimes favor one people over another, but the laws of physics treat us all the same.

No exceptions. ●

Words to Understand

infrared spectroscopy
a technique for using invisible, infrared light to interact with molecules and then create pictures of their movement

quanta
the smallest amount of something that can exist by itself, measured in a specific amount

Chapter 1

Elmer Imes

Born:
1883

Died:
1941

Nationality:
American

Achievements:
Leading early theorist
in light and
quantum physics.

magine the year 1915. The world was in the grip of World War I, but in the United States, the effects of a previous war—the Civil War—were still being felt. The Civil War had torn the country apart over the issues of slavery and the rights of black people. Although more than 50 years had passed, the United States was still divided in the early 20th century. Schools, restaurants, and hotels were segregated. In the South, there were laws passed to discriminate against black people. There were not many educational or professional pathways open to blacks, especially in a field like physics.

There were a few opportunities, however, and Elmer Imes was determined to take advantage of them. Both of his parents had gone to college, and he was raised in a household that valued education. By 1915, Imes had

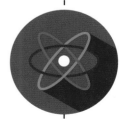

earned a bachelor's and master's degree in science from Fisk University, a historically black college in his hometown of Memphis, Tennessee. It was a good start, but the city of Memphis was in the South, the region of the country that was most hostile to blacks. Imes knew that he had to get the best education possible to excel in science and decided to attend a northern university to get his doctorate. He chose the University of Michigan, where he worked with many established and respected physicists and made a name for himself in the area of **infrared spectroscopy**.

For his doctoral work at Michigan, Imes designed and built spectrometers, devices that detect light waves. The machines used infrared light (a type of light wave that is invisible to people, and that we feel as heat) to create high-resolution pictures. These pictures showed how molecules were moving in certain gases. Molecules can move in two ways: they can vibrate along the bonds that link their atoms, and they can rotate around their center of gravity. Research had already shown that the energy in vibrational movements came in specific amounts called **quanta**. Imes's work would show that rotational movement also could be measured in quanta.

These breakthroughs were important to quantum theory, which was relatively new at the time. Even though there were established laws of physics, they did not always explain everything that scientists observed. Scientists wondered if quantum theory could explain physical occurrences that did not make sense using the laws of classical physics.

Like many in physics, Imes used high-level mathematics along with observation to create his theories and experiments.

But was quantum theory viable, or just a far-fetched idea? Imes's work was able to give scientists a way to test important parts of quantum theory, and now it is widely accepted.

Earle Plyler, another important physicist who pioneered work in infrared spectroscopy, said in a 1974 speech, "Imes's work formed a turning point in the scientific thinking, making it clear that quantum theory was not just a novelty, useful in [limited] field of physics, but of widespread and general application."

In 1918, Imes became only the second African American to get a doctoral degree in physics. He had proved he was a gifted scientist. Putting his talents to work in the job market was another hurdle he had to clear, as racism was

still standard in the United States. After finishing his doctoral work, Imes could not find a job teaching at a university; most colleges were still segregated. Colleges for white students did not want to hire a black professor, and most colleges for black students did not offer classes in physics. Imes had to find another way into a career in science. He moved to New York City, where he worked as a consultant and researcher for several companies. He helped develop devices and instruments that measured electrical and magnetic properties.

Imes spent most of his teaching career at Fisk University, located in Memphis, Tennessee.

After a decade in New York, Imes wanted to return to Memphis. In 1930 he took a job at his old school, Fisk, running the physics department. Imes knew how difficult it was for African Americans to establish themselves in the sciences. At Fisk, he set up a track for graduate level studies in physics, and helped his students find opportunities for an advanced education. Imes worked with invisible light in his laboratory, but the way he lit the path for his students was very visible. His pioneering work as a scientist, and his efforts on behalf of black students, are things we can still see today. ●

Words to Understand

conduct
to move or transport

electron
a negatively charged particle in an atom

friction
the resistance caused by two objects rubbing together

trajectory
a path with a specific direction

Chapter 2

Shirley Ann Jackson

Born:
1946

Nationality:
American

Achievements:
Work in electronics inspired
advances in semiconductors;
helped with nuclear cleanup

S hirley Ann Jackson had a need for speed. The Washington, D.C., neighborhood she grew up in was full of hills, and the children who lived there entertained themselves by building go carts from spare parts, and then racing them against each other. The fastest cart won, of course. Jackson wanted it to be hers.

The carts had no engines and did not use any fuel. Instead, they relied on gravity pulling them down hills. Jackson set to work figuring out how to use this to her advantage. She tried different things, and paid close attention to what worked and what didn't. What design was best? What materials were the most effective? Jackson discovered that she needed to build her cart with a narrow front that could plow through the air, like the prow of a ship through water. She found wheels and axles that spun freely and didn't

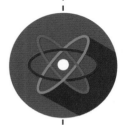

cause too much friction. At the beginning of the race, each cart got a first push to get it going. Where should she put the cart, to get the maximum amount of power from that push? All of this was physics at work, but Jackson wasn't thinking about that at the time—she just wanted to win the race!

Another race also had an influence on Jackson—the Space Race. After the Soviet Union put the satellite Sputnik into space in 1957, the United States was determined to catch up. It made its own space program a priority, which required talented scientists and engineers, so the country started emphasizing math and science in schools. Jackson was one of the first students to take advanced courses in these subjects. It was a great opportunity, especially because she was black and had spent her first years in segregated schools.

She went on to college at the Massachusetts Institute of Technology (MIT), a respected school for math and science. Jackson was only one of two African-American women in her class. She found there was still a lot of prejudice toward black

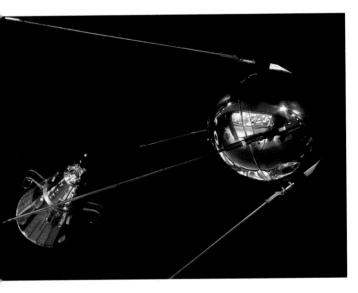

The launch of Sputnik by the U.S.S.R. in 1957 helped inspire Jackson to study physics.

Jackson did pioneering work in the makeup and materials of semiconductors, key components of electronic circuits.

people. "I decided the only way that I was going to succeed was to focus on physics and not on my race or gender," she says. "I let that be somebody else's problem." The strategy worked, and Jackson went on to get her Ph.D. in physics from MIT.

A few years later, she took a job with Bell Laboratories, a company that developed technologies for use in phones and other electronics. Jackson decided to study the behavior of **electrons** in two-dimensional (flat) materials. One thing she worked on was semiconductors. Semiconductors are an important component in computers and other electronics. They **conduct** electricity, but only under certain circumstances. Semiconductors are manufactured by putting thin layers of different materials together. As they build up, these layers can start to work against each other. If there is too much strain, it will damage the material. Jackson came up with mathematical ways to show how much strain the materials could handle. That way, they could be built with-

out having as many defects. Her work influences many of the objects we use today, such as CDs, DVDs, and optical scanners like the ones used to read price codes on items from the store.

A new opportunity came up in 1995. President Bill Clinton asked Jackson to be on the government commission that oversees nuclear power plants. Less than a decade earlier, a devastating nuclear accident had occurred at the Chernobyl plant in the Soviet Union and nuclear safety was on everyone's mind. Jackson was ideal for the

After serving on a national commission about nuclear power plants, Jackson became president of a major university.

job because she had knowledge of nuclear physics, plus a natural talent for leadership and communication. A few years later Jackson made another career move, becoming the president of Rensselaer Polytechnic Institute in New York, where she still is today. She had always fought to improve educational opportunities for women and African Americans and this position gives her even more influence. "Reach for the stars. It always gives you an upward **trajectory**," Jackson advises students. "If you do not reach, you do not get anywhere." ●

Shirley Ann Jackson:
Engineer-turned-college-president

Words to Understand

quantum mechanics
the scientific principles that describe how matter on a small scale
(such as atoms and electrons) behaves

string theory
a theory about how particles move and interact with each other

supersymmetry
an idea in particle physics in which each type of particle has a
corresponding partner

Chapter 3

Sylvester James Gates

Born:
1950

Nationality:
American

Achievements:
Theoretical physicist and leading educator

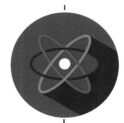

A ball rolling down a hill might not seem like very exciting stuff. To describe that event, you could say, "Well, there was this ball, and it rolled down a hill." Or you could use some more detailed information, like the distance the ball traveled and how long it took. That's what Jim Gates's high school physics teacher did. When he went on to show how those two things related mathematically, it seemed like a bit of magic to Gates. Up until then, he had thought of math as a type of game. It was like reading comic books or making up stories about superheroes. Math had rules, but in Gates's mind, those rules were just imaginary things that could be changed around. His teacher showed him that everyday happenings—balls rolling down hills—could be explained using math. It was a link Gates had not thought of before.

"I never got over that experience," he remembers. "I immediately said, 'That's what I want to do, because I know how to make up stuff real well. If I'm going to make up these mathematical games and some of them are actually going to be real, then what could be more fun?'"

It wasn't his first experience wondering about math and equations. Several years earlier, as a child, Gates had come across an equation in an encyclopedia. He knew it was math because of the plus and equal signs in it, but he did not understand the other symbols. Still, he knew it meant something. He wondered if one day, he *could* understand it. Gates now knows he was looking at the Schrödinger equation, which describes changes that happen in **quantum mechanics**. And yes, he understands it.

But there's plenty else he still doesn't understand. As a theoretical physicist at the University of Maryland, Gates studies the topics of **supersymmetry** and **string theory**. These are two related ideas in physics that deal with particles in matter and how they move. They have not been proved, but if they were—and that's a big if—they could help physicists explain some things.

Things like gravity, for example.

For decades, physicists have worked within what is called the Standard Model of Physics. There are four basic forces in physics. The laws in the Standard Model help explain three of them—electromagnetism, and the weak and strong interactions in nuclear forces. However, the fourth force—gravity—cannot be explained through the Standard Model.

The famous physicist Albert Einstein came up with the theory of general relativity. It was able to describe gravity in part, and is one of the most important theories of the 20th century. However, it does not fit into the Standard Model. Einstein wanted to find a theory that would encompass all the physical forces, all the time. Scientists today are still working on that. Such a theory would be called the Unified Field Theory, or "the theory of everything." Gates believes the answers could be wrapped up in supersymmetry and string theory.

German scientist Albert Einstein revolutionized physics in the early 20th century.

It's a pretty ambitious task, and Gates knows he might not even be alive to see if these theories turn out to be true. Instead, he says his contribution is to create the ideas and then put them out there, like a message in a bottle. Later generations may find them and have the knowledge that will help to decipher the message.

Gates admits that he spends a lot of time getting it wrong. "Most of the time, when we make up ideas, they're wrong. People think theoretical physicists are really bright and they can do all this amazing stuff, but most of what we do is just absolutely wrong. That's just the nature of innovation. However, when we get it right, it's amazing. That's what theoretical physics is all about." ●

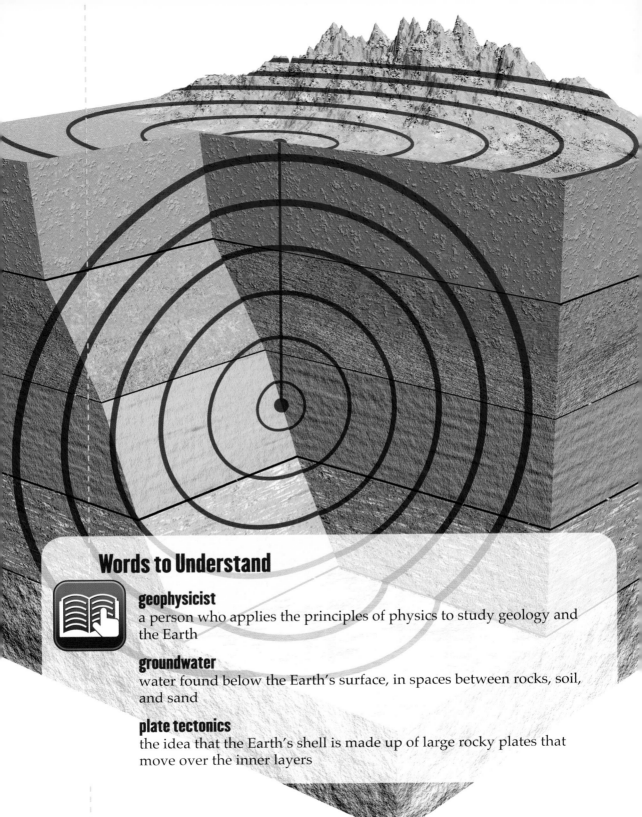

Words to Understand

geophysicist
a person who applies the principles of physics to study geology and the Earth

groundwater
water found below the Earth's surface, in spaces between rocks, soil, and sand

plate tectonics
the idea that the Earth's shell is made up of large rocky plates that move over the inner layers

Chapter 4

Estella Atekwana

Nationality:
Cameroonian

Achievements:
Geophysicist who
studies motion of plates
in the Earth to learn
about earthquakes

If you want to take a trip with Estella Atekwana, bring some good shoes. Expect to live in a tent much of the time. As a professor and a **geophysicist**, Atekwana studies the Earth itself. She often takes her students with her as she travels all over the world. Her work has taken her to the remote outback of western Australia, the Kalahari Desert in southern Africa, and the Gulf of Mexico off the coast of Louisiana. "My teaching style is to give students a strong theoretical background, and then a lot of hands-on experience," says Atekwana. "In the working world, theory is second to knowing how to process and interpret data. We are trying to take physics and math and make sense of the geology."

Atekwana was raised in Cameroon, a country in western Africa. Her parents wanted her to go into medicine, so she enrolled

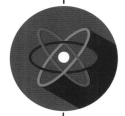

in science courses with that goal. A geology class in high school changed her course, however. Her teacher did not think Atekwana could handle the work because she was a girl. Atekwana took up the challenge. "I ended up with the science award that year in chemistry, biology, and geology," she remembers. She went on to get her bachelor's and master's degrees in geology. Then she topped off her education with a doctorate in geophysics, and now works at Oklahoma State University. "Today, they call me Doctor and that's fine with my parents," she says.

The Earth is in a constant state of change. Geophysicists study how those changes occur, and what effects they have.

Atekwana headed to the field to look at groundwater.

One of Atekwana's research interests is **plate tectonics**. Just as bones form the skeleton of the human body, there are large rocky plates on the Earth's outer layer that make up the planet's "bones." These plates are always in slow motion, moving past each other. They push together and pull apart. Atekwana studies how those plates shift over time, forming new land masses or opening up oceans.

Geophysicists also study forces such as gravity and magnetism. Those forces cause the Earth to look or behave in a certain way. Scientists can use this data in a number of ways. For example, they can locate resources in the earth, such as oil and natural gas. This information also helps engineers determine how to dig it up.

After she started her career, Atekwana found herself pioneering a new field called biogeophysics. In the mid-1990s, she was part of a team that studied an area that had been contaminated with oil. The team took measurements of the **groundwater** in the area, and found the water conducted electricity better than normal water. They traced the reason to microbes, tiny organisms that lived in the water. When the water became contaminated, the microbes started breaking down the oil. As they did, they released chemically charged particles. Those made the water more able to conduct electricity. "We [saw] that microorganisms can significantly impact the physical properties of their environment," Atekwana explains. "Biogeophysics was born." Several years later, Atekwana studied a massive oil spill that happened in the Gulf of Mexico in 2011.

She's also looked for evidence of microbes in Australia. Organisms that lived long ago may have left their mark in the soil. Their geophysical signatures could show scientists how to look for signs of life on other planets, such as Mars.

Microbes and physics may not seem like they have much in common. However, the way that microbes work together leaves a mark on the Earth. It's similar to how people—no matter what their color—can work together to make changes. "We could learn a lot from them," she says. "If we weren't spending so much time fighting about our differences, [we could learn] how our differences complement each other." ●

Words to Understand

brane world
a theory that says there are more than three dimensions of space

mentor
a person who provides encouragement and advice to those with less experience

Chapter 5

Arlie Petters

Born:
1964

Nationality:
Belizean/American

Achievements:
Mathematical physicist
who studies black
holes and other
celestial phenomena

I t takes a confident person to become one of the great thinkers of history, and that is one of the qualities Arlie Petters admires about physicist Albert Einstein. "He was not afraid to go into the unknown, intellectually," says Petters. Einstein is known for coming up with the idea that space and time are related. That meant the universe had four dimensions: three dimensions of space, and one of time. It was a revolutionary theory that transformed how physicists saw the world.

Even the great thinkers must be challenged, though. Petters, who is a mathematical physicist at Duke University, thinks Einstein's theories might need some updating. Since Einstein's time, some scientists have theorized that four dimensions might not be enough. They believe there could be five dimensions—or even more.

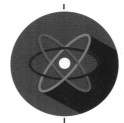

This is the idea behind the **brane world** theory. "Brane" is short for membrane. The theory is that our universe is actually like a three-dimensional membrane that floats inside another dimension. It is difficult to understand because people are used to only three dimensions of space. "Imagine if you live on the surface of a sheet of paper, and you can't get off it," Petters explains. "How do you know there's such a thing as *off* the sheet of paper? We cannot come out of length, width, and height. Even saying that sounds a little crazy."

This artist's conception of a black hole shows how its powerful gravity sucks in all matter around it.

Maybe so, but Petters is working to see if it's true.

His research involves black holes, huge, dark areas in space that have incredibly strong gravity. When light passes by a black hole, the gravity bends the light waves and distorts what we see. It is similar to looking through a magnifying glass or a strong pair of glasses. This effect is called gravitational lensing.

Petters thinks the universe—and even our solar system—may contain "mini" black holes. He has developed a mathematical theory that may be able to prove how and where gravitational lensing is happening. It would show that these black holes exist. If they do, "It would confirm that there is a fourth dimension to space," he says. "[That] would create a philosophical shift in our understanding of the natural world."

Petters's journey to the fifth dimension began in a much simpler place. He grew up in a small village in the Central American country of Belize. Electricity was not widespread, and there weren't very many books. Petters read what he could find by the light of a kerosene lamp.

Petters theorizes that gravity bends much like light bends through a magnifying glass.

Back home in Belize, a tropical land on the Gulf of Mexico, Petters has started an institute to encourage young scientists.

Overhead, though, there was plenty of light. Petters spent hours gazing into the night sky, wondering why the stars twinkled. Later, he was fascinated by the beauty of mathematical patterns. These things worked together to convince him he wanted to go into science.

Petters moved to New York as a teenager. There he found a **mentor** who helped him get into a program for minority students at Hunter College. Petters graduated, and then went on to get a Ph.D. from (MIT). Now, he works to be a mentor to other young students. He often gets emails from students who want to know what his career is like. He always answers them, because it reminds him of when a famous black mathematician once answered his letter.

He has also opened the Petters Research Institute in his native Belize. Its purpose is to give kids opportunities to explore math and science. "This grand reality is there for all of us, rich or poor," says Petters. "No one [has] any special privileges to it. We are all in the same boat in the face of the mystery of existence!" ●

Arlie Petters:
Investigating black holes

Words to Understand

ion
an atom that has a positive or negative electrical charge, depending on the number of electrons

nanometer
a measurement of length that is one-billionth of a meter

Chapter 6

Edward Thomas

Born:
1967

Nationality:
American

Achievements:
Studies plasma physics,
the motion of the
unusual state of matter in
space and in nature

You've heard of solids, liquids, and gases—three different states of matter. Plasma is a fourth type of matter. It does not get as much attention, but it's actually the most common form of visible matter in nature. Some 99 percent of what we can see is plasma!

On Earth, flames and lightning bolts are types of plasma. So are auroras, a kind of light in the sky that is produced when solar winds blow through the atmosphere. Plasmas can also be man-made. Fluorescent lights, computer chips, and televisions all use plasma technology. The place where plasmas really shine, though, isn't our planet. It's space. The rings of Saturn, the long tails of comets, and most stars—including our Sun—are all forms of plasma.

A plasma is a gas that has an electrical charge. The charges of atoms are determined

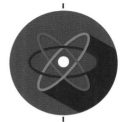

by the number of protons and electrons they have. Protons have a positive charge. Electrons have a negative one. Most of the time they balance each other out, and an atom is neutral. When there is more of one or the other, the atom becomes an **ion**, meaning it has a charge. When there are more protons than electrons, it is positive. If there are more electrons, it is negative. When a gas gets hot enough, the energy causes some electrons to separate off from atoms. The gas becomes charged, turning it into a plasma.

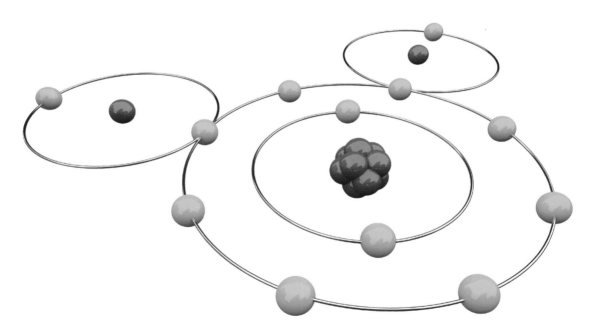

This model of water shows that its components include one large atom of oxygen and two smaller ones of hydrogen.

A "dusty" plasma takes all this one step farther. It adds in tiny particles, sometimes only **nanometers** big. (Take a strand of hair, and divide its diameter by 100,000. That's a nanometer.) These particles become electrically charged as well. They interact with the atoms and free-roaming electrons in the plasma, and can influence how the whole thing flows.

For Edward Thomas, this dust is nothing to sneeze at. A professor of plasma physics, Thomas is researching how dusty plasmas behave. Using a huge, 6,000-pound magnet that can actually control the magnetic field, Thomas hopes

This plasma ball device lets viewers see this unusual substance in action.

to manage how the dust moves and collects in the plasma. He wants to study how energy causes particles to move in a plasma. Then people might be able to harness that energy. "If we can control the behavior of dust, then we can see how to use dust as a tool," he says.

Thomas grew up on the island of Saint Thomas, part of the US Virgin Islands. He always wanted to be a scientist, but he really fell in love with it during the summer between eighth and ninth grades. That's when his uncle, a marine biologist, took him to the Woods Hole Oceanographic Institute, an important research facility in Massachusetts.

The Sun is the source of some plasma. The blob at bottom right is a huge jet of plasma being ejected from the Sun.

The projects going on there were interesting, but what really stuck with Thomas was how the scientists were so excited about their work. Thomas still had not settled on any particular area of science, but watching the people there convinced him of one thing. "I firmly believe that whatever you want to do, you have to be passionate about it," he says.

He went on to study physics in college, getting his doctorate from Auburn University in Alabama, where he now works. In addition to studying dusty plasmas in the lab, he also observes how plasma behaves in space. Most of the time, plasma waves roll through space without interference. Near

Earth, however, they can crash into satellite equipment. This throws off the satellites' communication signals. Thomas's work may help scientists get a better handle on how plasma moves through space. Then they can design equipment that could mean better signals for satellite phones and GPS systems.

Physics is filled with challenges, and Thomas has made his share of mistakes. The key was learning from the mistakes, and applying it to new challenges. He tells students to adapt what they learn to new circumstances, and to take advantage of opportunities. "There are many, many exciting projects out there—take the time to explore as many as you can to find one that you like!" ●

Words to Understand

macroscopic
on a large scale, as opposed to microscopic (small)

pipette
a small dropper (similar to an eyedropper) used for measuring liquids
in a laboratory

Chapter 7

Nadya Mason

Born:
1973

Nationality:
American

Achievements:
Studies condensed
matter physics and how
electrons move in
graphene; also works
in nanotechnolgy

For Nadya Mason, doing science experiments is no big deal. It's all about the little things, actually.

The *very* little things, like a few nanometers wide.

Scientists have known for a while that materials behave differently based on their size. As a physics professor at the University of Illinois, Mason does research to figure out what exactly is happening with extremely small particles—and why.

As a child, Mason loved math and science. She spent hours working math puzzles, and liked to be out in nature. "I was one of those kids who loved running around, picking fruits off of trees and poking at ant hills and seeing what the caterpillars were doing on any given summer day," she says. She was also a competitive gymnast, and almost—but not quite—made the US national team that

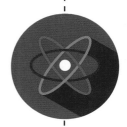

went to the Olympics. In high school she decided it was time to focus on either gymnastics or science. She chose the challenge of science. "I realized you could just play around the lab, use **pipettes** and put things in beakers. You could just think your way through what you were doing." She liked physics in particular. "Physics really described the world in a way that I wanted to understand it. It made sense to me."

She was able to do internships at a local university and company. One was in biochemistry and one was in

All these food items are made of matter, but they each exist in different states from liquid to solid.

geophysics. "From these experiences I realized that I loved experimental science, but that I did not want to do biochemistry or geophysics!" she says. "Sometimes it's as important to gain experience to figure out what you *don't* want to do, as it is to figure out what you *do* want to do."

This model shows the microscopic structure of graphene.

What she wanted turned out to be experimental condensed matter physics. Basically, condensed matter is stuff—solids and liquids. Cardboard and cans, spoons and snow, orange juice and honey—they're all condensed matter. The physics of condensed matter explains why cardboard gets soggy in water but cans don't. It explains why a spoon can hold a heaping pile of snow, but will overflow when the snow melts into water. It explains why orange juice pours easily but honey sticks to the jar.

These are large, three-dimensional substances, however. Mason works with a two-dimensional material called graphene. Graphene is a very thin sheet of carbon atoms connected together in a lattice structure (similar to a window screen.) It is only one atom thick. Roll up a piece of graphene and it becomes a carbon nanotube. Now it looks like the skinniest wire you can imagine.

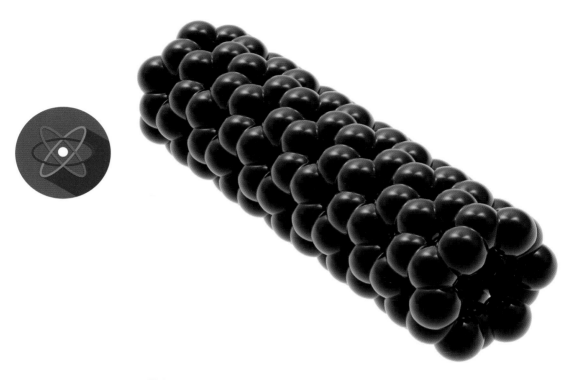

This is a model of a carbon nanotube, formed by manipulating graphene in interesting ways.

Mason studies how electrons move around in graphene, and how that affects its electrical conductivity. It turns out that in the flat world of carbon nanotubes, electrons start doing unusual things. Their movement is dominated by the theories of quantum mechanics. This is a set of equations that show how extremely tiny particles move and interact with each other.

"Electrons act very differently when they're scaled down to very small sizes," Mason explains. "You start getting something that's in between atomic physics, of single atoms, and physics. In this area you start to see a crossover between quantum effect and macrosopic effect."

Mason's discoveries could be important for a number of technologies that people use every day. "[It could] be very relevant to the computer industry, which has a stake in making computers keep working no matter how small they get," says Mason. Although today's computers are pretty fast, the quantum computers of tomorrow could be much faster. These electrons may not travel very far, but they could mean a big leap forward in physics technology. ●

Nadya Mason:
Peering into nanotechnology

Words to Understand

dyslexia
a type of disorder that makes reading difficult

Maggie Aderin-Pocock

Born:
1968

Nationality:
British

Achievements:
Astrophysicist, TV host,
and proponent of science
careers for young women

Imagine climbing to the top of a tall tree, where it's possible to see everything happening for miles around. Now peer down to the ground, where you can just barely see a group of ants, furiously fighting over a tiny bit of food. Compared with the view from the top of the tree, the ants probably don't seem that important in the whole scheme of things.

Now take this idea a little further. If you look out at the whole universe, you might decide that people fighting on Earth isn't all that important. That's what Maggie Aderin-Pocock thinks. As a black, female scientist, she has faced a lot of adversity in her career. For her, the solution was to focus on things that have nothing to do with race or gender. "I've always been fascinated by space—it seems to transcend all human problems," she says.

Real space, fake space—Aderin-Pocock

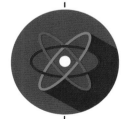

loved it all when she was growing up in London, England, the daughter of Nigerian parents. She gazed up at the stars in the sky, and she watched a British TV show called *The Clangers* about mice who lived on another planet. As a young child, Aderin-Pocock wanted to be an astronaut and visit the mice. That hasn't worked out yet, but today, as a space scientist with a background in physics, she has found other ways to get into space.

At school, Aderin-Pocock struggled with reading and writing because she has dyslexia. However, she excelled at math and science. Her father had wanted to become a doctor, and he encouraged his daughter to do the same. However, Aderin-Pocock found she was more interested in physics than medicine. Her dream was to spin out brilliant theories like Albert Einstein. Then she discovered that she was more suited to practical, hands-on work. As a teenager, she took a class where she built her own telescope. "It was fantastic because I made it with my own hands, and it got me closer to the stars I loved."

She went on to get degrees in physics and mechanical engineering, and went to work for the British government. One of her first jobs was to create a missile warning system to alert pilots. Her passion remained with space science though, so next she took a job with the team that was building the Gemini Telescope country of Chile. It's difficult to study stars that are billions of miles away, but one method is to observe their light patterns. Aderin-Pocock helped design a spectrograph for the telescope. This instrument

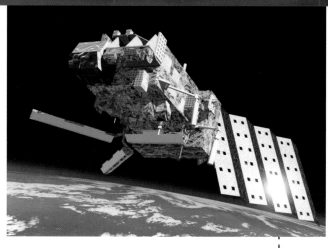

isolates light waves according to their frequencies. Scientists then analyze the types of light that stars give off.

She switched from making instruments based on Earth to making ones that go up in space. She helps build special systems for satellites. These systems measure conditions in the Earth's atmosphere, such as wind speeds. This data can help scientists study climate change. "Doing physics and mechanical engineering turned out to be the perfect marriage for making satellites," she says.

The MetOp-A satellite launched by the European Space Agency is one of many studying Earth's climate.

Aderin-Pocock hasn't given up her goal of going into space, but currently she's focused on getting more minority kids with science. She gives talks at schools and on TV to show how science is open to everyone. "Physics careers are not very visible. I have been trying to show people, show black kids, that to be a scientist isn't an odd thing," she says. "You don't need a big brain the size of a planet. You need a passion to understand things." ●

Maggie Aderin-Pocock:
Making science for everyone

NASA astronaut and medical doctor,
Mae Jemison

Careers in Physics

Tr here are plenty of things that people can change, but the laws of physics are not among them. We can't travel faster than the speed of light. We can't create energy. The human body is not strong enough to jump out of the Earth's gravity. It might seem that the laws of physics are pretty limiting! What people can do is learn more about those laws. Then we can use them to help us do things.

Take rocket science. Rocket fuel has a lot of energy, but sprinkling it on a rocket won't do any good. Instead, rocket scientists figured out how to design a machine that would transfer that energy into mechanical motion. Humans still can't travel faster than light, but they did escape Earth's gravity to go into space! The work of physicists has given us computers, televisions, phones, satellites, and X-ray machines.

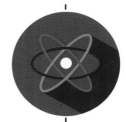

Physicists today are peering deeper and deeper into molecules and atoms. They are finding the tiniest particles imaginable and observing what they do. The laws of physics have been in place since the beginning of time. That does not mean that scientists know what all the laws are, or how they work. Bit by bit, though, the scientific discoveries are changing how we see the world and how we live in it.

It might be intimidating to think about pursuing a career in physics. After all, who could compete with the likes of Isaac Newton or Albert Einstein? Fortunately, there is

Studying the physical properties of chemicals and how they interact with matter is a starting point for some physics students.

room for a lot of different people, and a lot of different ways of thinking. Science always needs creative minds to come up with new ideas and challenge old ones.

Historically, blacks and other minorities have had fewer opportunities to pursue science in middle school or high school. By the time they get to college, they sometimes believe that science is too difficult. In addition, black youths do not see many people of color in the sciences. According to data from the American Institute of Physics, just over 2 percent of physics faculty members in the United States are black. That's a lot less than the 13 percent of black people in the country overall. Without role models to guide them, many blacks simply choose different careers.

Society is changing, slowly, but in the meantime, students of any race who are interested in a career in physics can take steps to get there. First is education. The study of physics affects every kind of science. Biology, chemistry, astronomy, geology, oceanography, and others rely on the principles of physics. Getting a broad knowledge of the sciences is helpful to understanding how physics applies in different fields. It's also important to take as much math as possible. Physicists like Jim Gates and Arlie Petters recognized that math was a "language" of its own—and that it was the only language people had that could describe physics.

What does a physicist do all day? You might get an image of someone standing at a blackboard covered in complicated equations. Although that's part of physics, there's a lot more to it. Science isn't all books. Doing hands-on

work can let students get a feel for what working in the field is like. Many colleges offer internships for high school students so they can learn from professionals. These internships can also help you determine what environments you like to work in, and what parts of the sciences interest you most—or least. For Nadya Mason, her internships in science showed her what she did *not* want to do!

Careers in physics can be very hands on, as the theories of how light, motion, and matter work are turned into real-life products.

Finding a mentor can be especially helpful. Because there are relatively few blacks in scientific professions, someone who has been through the process can offer an insider's perspective and offer advice about how to face challenges.

There is no specific industry called "physics." People with physics degrees can work in all types of different fields, from computer science to engineering. Although many physics professionals work at colleges and universities, doing research and teaching classes, many more are employed elsewhere. Elmer Imes, Shirley Ann Jackson, and Maggie Aderin-Pocock all put their talents to work in government or industry jobs. For example, space programs in the United States and abroad need physicists to build equipment and study astronomy. Private companies also hire physicists to work on different projects such as designing aircraft, medical equipment, and electronics. These types of jobs have a strong focus on engineering, as well. The theories of physics are applied to make and improve products that people use.

Physicists often say that their best skill is the ability to solve problems. They take what they do know and put it to work on what they don't. They gaze up at stars, watch balls roll down hills, and ask questions about how the world works. Then they do the fun part—finding the answers. ●

Text-Dependent Questions

1. What are two ways that molecules move?

2. What does a semiconductor do?

3. Which physical force cannot be explained using the Standard Model of physics?

4. Why are scientists looking for a Unified Field Theory?

5. How can microbes make water conduct electricity better?

6. What happens when light passes by a black hole?

7. How much of the visible universe is plasma?

8. What are the two ways that nuclear power is created?

9. What is graphene?

10. Early in the history of the universe, electrons got pulled off hydrogen atoms. What was this process called?

Suggested Research Projects

1. Physicists study the properties of light to observe how particles move. Investigate the light spectrum to find out how physicists use data from light to gather information.

2. Look up different designs for cars or other vehicles. Note some of the ways you think the principles of physics were used to make them faster or more efficient.

3. Plate tectonics have been shaping the Earth for billions of years, and scientists believe Earth used to look very different. Research the land masses and oceans on the planet during different eras.

4. The Hubble Space Telescope has taken hundreds of pictures of objects in space that show the effects of gravitational lensing. Look some up to see what this amazing phenomenon looks like.

5. Computers, TVs, and phones use conductors, semiconductors, and insulators to manage electrical signals. Find out how these parts work together to make electronic machines work properly.

6. Climate change is one of the biggest environmental problems on Earth. Find out some of the ways physics can be used to collect climate data.

Find Out More

Websites

www.ducksters.com/science/physics/
Check out this site for links to lots of different areas of physics, such as motion, electricity, astronomy, and light and sound.

www.physics.org/careers.asp?contentid=381
This site has some great stories of physicists and their jobs. Find out what they do all day!

www.physicscentral.com/
Ask questions, find experiments, and research tons of topics in physics through this website.

Books

Field, Andrea R., ed. *The Science of Physics*. New York: Rosen Publishing, 2011.
A look at some of the basic principles used in physics.

Gilliland, Ben. *Rocket Science for the Rest of Us*. London: DK Children, 2015.
An introductory book about rocket science, astronomy, astrophysics, and space travel.

Series Glossary of Key Terms

botany the study of plant biology

electron a negatively charged particle in an atom

genome all the DNA in an organism, including all the genes

nanometer a measurement of length that is one-billionth of a meter

nanotechnology manipulation of matter on an atomic or molecular scale

patent a set of exclusive rights granted to an inventor for a limited period of time in exchange for detailed public disclosure of an invention

periodic table the arrangement of all the known elements into a table based on increasing atomic number

protein large molecules in the body responsible for the structure and function of all the tissues in an organism

quantum mechanics the scientific principles that describe how matter on a small scale (such as atoms and electrons) behaves

segregated separated, in this case by race

ultraviolet a type of light, usually invisible, that can cause damage to the skin

Index

Photo credits

About the Author

Diane Bailey has written about 50 nonfiction books for kids and teens, on topics ranging from science to sports to celebrities. She also works as a freelance editor, helping authors who write novels for children and young adults. Diane has two sons and two dogs, and lives in Kansas.